REMAKE

CHANGE THE WAY YOU THINK, ACT, & LIVE.

HARISH REDDY S

ᗒᗒᗒ

Dedicated to all of us, in changing our perspectives of everything
which we blindly believe in just because everyone believes

ᗒᗒᗒ

Contents

Contents

Preface

My passion for writing originates from my desire to express both the positive and negative stuff that exists within us and all around us. And purposefully proposing my opinions and ideas to my readers in order to assist them in creating the life they desire, by compelling the content in the World about what is what and what is not what.

The greatest question is
How we perceive our surroundings influences who we are as individuals. If we only depended on our own perceptions to determine the truth, we would surely have a confused sense of reality. However, we cannot see the complete spectrum of options or comprehend them clearly.

To put it another way, we're all too limited to make our own decisions.

As a result, I believe that relying on outside facts is the most logical way to form our opinions.

A wise man once said."***We have a tendency to believe what we want to believe and ignore the rest***". It's because we always believe what we believe is correct, we draw our own conclusions, or by just following the mass majority.

You alone have the power to rethink the beliefs and can rewrite it, and this would give you more confidence in your conclusions.

A bit more clearly I can say is that
Your life is based on perspectives, Everyday you have a new lesson to learn, your everyday starts with different story, and your everyday end with different ending and everyday you see different people with different lives, beliefs, attitudes, and experiences. Thereafter you'll realize there are many stories and so many endings and we are just part of this cycle of beginning of our birth and departure of death, and what we do, how we live, how we think has a lot of impact on our own lives as well as on others, The relationships we build, the knowledge we gain, the success we

achieve, and the love we express must all be based on living a life correctly and genuinely.

If you question yourself after every little thing you do, if you try to understand your actions and decide on them, and that's how you conclude everything right, being able to live life in a right way is considered weak and false to this accused world. Because in this suspect false world, people do not believe the truth of one, but the false of many.

ᗺᗺᗺ

Author Bio

Harish Reddy s is an Indian non-fiction author and as well as he recently completed his master's degree in master of Business Administration, his latest book was Twelve magical stairs towards success. Son of Srinivasa Reddy & Chandramma, born and raised in Karnataka in the Kolar district, and currently lives in Bangalore.

Let's Get Social

Instagram: author_harishreddy

Twitter: harishreddysss

E-Mail: authorharishreddy@gmail.com

ᖺᖺᖺ

Introduction

Learning new things is essential to living, but so is slavishly adhering to some unquestionable views just because everyone else does. **Our thoughts and judgments are disregarded by the family or society when we try to alter anything by questioning it.**

Everyone needs to have their own thoughts and convictions; *else, you risk becoming simply another person who follows the herd.*

Respect yourself and your right to speak up for what you believe in.

That being said, there are instances when it is important to challenge the ideas of others, just so long as you can support your own convictions with logic and reason. However, if your objective is to advance in life, it's typically preferable to go with the flow. Always think for yourself but behave for the majority, until you are in a position of a higher power. But just don't be a mindless follower that blindly follows everyone else.

Thoughts have great power. They may be productive or destructive, positive or negative. Our thoughts about ourselves and the world around us **have an impact on our words and deeds, which in turn mold our routines and way of life.**

It's important to pay attention to our thoughts and weed out any negative ones. We may achieve this by swapping them out with helpful, uplifting ideas. To develop healthy habits and a healthy lifestyle, our words and deeds should be in harmony with our optimistic ideas.

With this technology of the modern world, Our lives today are one of infinite possibilities.

Today, you are more than just one person.

One of a million choices and paths.

One of infinite personalities and angles, that can be combined and customized to you. Who needs to be " just one person or to live with just one identity?" when you have no restrictions to be anyone or anything you want to be???

The majority of us know what to do. Moreover, we simply follow the same old advice that our elders, friends, and even self-help books have given us countless times.

But how many of us actually follow them?

We rarely follow the same advice that we give others. Sometimes we even make things more complicated. It is simple. We have been doing so since we are habituated to doing so.

We do not have the habit to take action.

We do not have the habit to think we can improve ourselves.

We do not have the habit to embrace the best things in our life.

It's a tragedy that in a world full of opportunities, there are so many people with great potential who are yet invisible to the world.

Unfortunately, many people with **amazing skills and abilities are never given the chance to shine.** It's heartbreaking, whether it's because they come from **a poor background or because they lack the contacts or finances** to get their foot in the door.

It's not about knowing certain aspects of life without understanding whether they're right or wrong. It's about understanding you've been living your life without understanding yourself, your surroundings, or the people and substances around you. It's about understanding that in a universe of infinite possibilities,

You know everything, yet exist as NOTHING!

ᔭᔭᔭ

Foreword

SHREYA PILLAI & AVINASH KUMAR SINGH

ᐅᐅᐅ

Shreya Pillai

Harish Reddy's works generally focus on the working and wielding of the mind and mind power. In his book, 'Twelve Magical Stairs towards Success' he'd thoroughly described the motivation and the impetus required to mold your lifestyle to fit in with your idea of 'success'. Oftentimes we as human beings confirm ourselves within the boundaries of narrow, constricted mindsets that keep us imprisoned in a state of mediocrity and a sense of unworthiness. While the author cannot make each and every one of you readers invoke the feeling to stop limiting yourselves to standards and mindsets, his words can definitely make you think. You might want to pick this book up if you're someone who believes in yourself and the sheer untapped potential you hold within the bounds of yourself. This work is more than just a set of words bound within pages. This is a sensation. A subtle motivation, a push that you require to start somewhere, to aspire, and to inspire.

>**Shreya Pillai**
>
>**(Instagram - my_fair_fiction)**

ᐅᐅᐅ

Avinash Kumar Singh

I am delighted to write this foreword, not only because Mr. Harish Reddy S is a good friend of mine but also because writing this will actually remake my strength with words. Remake itself justifies how important it is to change within your life.

There are a lot of possibilities and ways to remake yourself. It has been seen in a society that people fight with themselves in search to be good and self-dependent. They often come out with the best or fail with the odds of their moves. We, humans, have a perspective that sometimes changing ourselves is a risky game and sometimes it's very hard to change. Remember the change is all about the direction and steps you step throughout. We have suggestions, ideas, and advice from elders, friends, or a self-help book but we still face a lot of difficulties to follow them.

What you need is proper guidance or a proper mindset to make the best out of these struggles. You have to prove that these efforts to remake yourself are actually worth it. In this entire journey, when you fight with yourself (your character), you need to be patient and clear with the vision. It's not a complicated job, it's so simple that people often make a mess out of it, just in search of some ease. Remaking should be in our habit and we should stick to it. Already we know that -

- We do not have a habit to remake ourselves.
- We never think that we can improve or turn out better.
- We don't know how to make the best out of a mess.

Everyone has an opportunity in their life. It never knocks on your door; you have to open it and grab it. It asks for your attention and efforts. Your life demands a remake from you. Take inspiration from the people who succeed while doing this. You need to develop a skill that suits your artwork best. You need a base that supports your entire work for an infinitely long time.

We know that many people do not have a stage to show off their talents and shine on their dashboards. Somehow their financial condition or poor background doesn't let them into this race. Remake yourself to be front for them. Bless them with the good heart you have and show how kind your whole nation should be. Remake deals with these important aspects and social values of human beings.

The remake has some basic chapters that will convey the importance of remaking and why it's so crucial to be discussed. The author has designed this book in a manner that would make you so comfortable with the area of remaking. Step into the world of change and learn how to connect with it. I hope this book will convey to you what it has been written for so long. Reading this book you'll find how important it is to change for yourself, for your friends, and for our nation. **Change for the right, fight for the right and live for the right.**

Avinash Kumar Singh
(Author and poet of romantic)

ᐅᐅᐅ

Acknowledgements

The world is great because of the people who valued the concepts I wrote down. As a self-published author, every reader who holds this book gets a particular thank you from the author, my holy spirit of Lord Ganesha, and my parents, who were proud and happy for my efforts. And a special thanks to my buddy Shivani Gudeeti, a true gem in my life, and Renuka E for her insignificant contribution to this thrill.

ᘖᘖᘖ

CHANGE THE WAY YOU THINK!

ONE
MINDSET

YOU is not you, You're the HEAD!

To escape the ordinary?

The start is to Think, Act & live the life you wanted. and everything is primarily commanded by your head.

You are solely in charge of your lifestyle, appearance, knowledge level, happiness level, and other aspects of your life.

As I believe that an individual who can create a link between their ambitions and realities is a successful.

The More Power You Have Over Your Life, The More Control You Have Over Your Outcome.

Often we wished to control our life as we wanted to live, right?

but sometimes we don't know what to do & how to do that. We want to make our own decisions, but we cannot because it's challenging when everyone around us is suggesting and filtering the best choices for us.

We can't just get rid of these people because they could be our friends and family and they really care about us & sometimes their words do manifest in our lives, but still there are some ways that you can take back control of your life.

- First of all get rid yourself of any unhealthy relationships you have in your life so they can no longer take part to influence your life.

- Determine what it is that one thing that you're truly desire to do with your life, and then get busy and pursue it.
- Make sure from the base of your soul that the choices you make are the choices you are completely satisfied with.

You must first think to decide something to pursue as well as for living a content life, primarily defined by the finest of our thought's. To be rich?, to be wealthy?, or to be famous or what so ever you want to achieve the start is to THINK.

𖠁𖠁𖠁

To Change Your Life? Change Your Thoughts, Perspectives, Your Conclusions & Many Other That Comes Along...

You won't ever come across a positive answer if you are always searching for the negative. You'll remain fixed in the same position if you believe that everything must be flawless. You will remain in the same place if you think things are beyond your control and that you don't have a solution to change them.

Starting with your ideas can help you alter your life. You may increase your prospects by thinking more positively and letting go of the negative ones. When faced with difficulty, don't concentrate on what you lack and the flaws in the circumstance. Instead, concentrate on what you can do to improve the situation and how to move ahead.

For example, if you feel that finding a good job is impossible, you will almost certainly end up with a poor one. If you feel that finding a good job is achievable, you are more likely to receive one.

Changing your perspectives is another method to improve your life.

For example, if you believe that the world is against you, the world is extremely likely to be against you. However, if you believe that the world is on your side, the world is more likely to be on your side. So, in short, we can alter our lives by altering our ideas and perceptions. And, of course, we can transform our lives by working hard and taking action.

❦❦❦

In Our Existence, Nothing Is Hard, The Only Hardest Thing That We Forget To Believe In Is Believing In Ourselves.

- *Nothing is impossible.* It's just that when you believe it to be so, it becomes that way.
- *Nothing is doubtful.* It's just that when you assume it to be so, it becomes that way.
- *Nothing is surreal.* It's just that when you allow it to become so, it does.

Believe in your dreams and see them through to completion.

Do not give up on something you are passionate about. Never doubt your abilities, and never let anyone convince you differently. You are capable of far more than anyone could ever imagine; your powers are far beyond what you believe you are capable of.

❦❦❦

Everyone's Success Is Delayed or Dismantled Due To A Lack Of Not Knowing Their Own Self-Course. If You Are In A Stage Of Life Where You Feel You Aren't Happy, You Have To Research, Realize And Remake That Something Which Is Bothering You.

what you are (A personal Self-help book titled *TWELVE MAGICAL STAIRS TOWARDS SUCCESS authored by HARISH REDDY S*, let you analyze and make you realize who you are and how to set up yourself towards success) can assist you in determining what you want, who you are, and where you want to go in life. Once this is completed, making judgments and taking action becomes much easier. The more honest you are with yourself, the better your decisions will be, and you will have greater success as a result.

The way we live our lives should be consistent with who we are at our basic, soul level. Being honest and Understanding ourselves for who we are is the first step towards being able to take command of our own lives and making them as satisfying as possible.

When we are not true to ourselves, we are continually seeking something that does not connect with who we actually are at our soul level. Because we are not living completely and genuinely, sometimes we may feel dead and even unhappy. We are missing out on all of the fantastic opportunities that may come our way because we are being false or trying to squeeze something into a box that does not fit us in any way.

ᚦᚦᚦ

Becoming Who You Are When No One Is Looking Is More Important Than Simply Being What You Want To Be. It's About Being Authentic. It's About Being Honest With Yourself

We all have times when we question if things will work out for us. It might be scary to feel as if you don't know what's going to happen next? and it's natural to be worried about your present situation. But, there are things you can do to get yourself out of depression so you may find your way and continue to improve as an individual.

One of the very first tasks is to determine what you want from life. You may have a vision or a dream that you want to see come true, but it is important that you identify those targets so that you can work toward them. Set some realistic deadlines once you've decided what you're searching for so you know when you need to act on your goals. This will assist you in remaining motivated and disciplined throughout the journey.

Another thing you may do is examine your strengths and weaknesses to understand more about yourself. What do you enjoy doing? What are your weaknesses? These are important questions to ask yourself, and you should start paying attention to how you feel in various situations and environments so you can respond correctly.

ᚦᚦᚦ

ϷϷϷ

This is a small story to make you realize how your thinking impacts your life.

Two men visit a **Zen master.**

The first man says: "I'm thinking of moving to this town. What's it like?"

The Zen master asks: "What was your old town like?"

The first man responds: "It was dreadful. Everyone was hateful. I hated it."

The Zen master says: "This town is very much the same. I don't think you should move here."

The first man leaves and the second man comes in.

The second man says: "I'm thinking of moving to this town. What's it like?"

The Zen master asks: "What was your old town like?"

The second man responds: "It was wonderful. Everyone was friendly and I was happy. Just interested in a change now."

The Zen master says: "This town is very much the same. I think you will like it here."

I like to think that the two men were from the same place every time I read the story. Changing your viewpoint is the simplest approach to making your life better. Does that mean it's always the best option? I'm not sure. But you should definitely give it a go first.

ϷϷϷ

You May Not Be Better Than Everyone But Again Not Everyone Is Better Than You.

It is the most amazing rule to live by. It will get you to the top, ahead of everyone else. You can be an average or even a bad person. But if you know who you are, what you are capable of, what your strengths are, and how you can use them to succeed, then you'll be better than many others. **You might not be the best in everything but you can be the best at what you're doing.**

In a world where mediocrity reigns, it is important to be exceptional.

You must understand that there's only one success and there are a million forms of failures. And the truth is that time destroys almost everything, so we must invest time in things that really matter and stay focused. The problem with many people is that they spend their time on things that don't matter.

 የየየ

To Think Differently?, Is To Find A Solution To Our Humanitarian Global Problems.

We must begin thinking differently if we are to discover solutions to the humanitarian issues facing the entire world. The conventional methods of thinking that initially caused these issues need to be abandoned. We must be receptive to fresh, creative ways of thinking that can lead us to novel answers.

We must think creatively and unconventionally to find innovative solutions that tackle the underlying causes of these issues.

We must consider the long term as well as the immediate future. We must consider the needs of all individuals, not just a select few.

So for all the possibilities, everyone says:

Everyone says to think differently,

Everyone says to think outside the box,

Everyone says to do that, do this, be that, & be this, and many continue with the flow...

But no one has the answer when we reply with a question mark of HOW?

How to think differently?

How to think Outside Of That Box?

How to do that, how to do this, how to be that, how to be this?

Everyone makes suggestions for you and uses quotes to inspire you, but no one ever sends you a letter with detailed instructions on how to think differently or outside the box.

An Everyday word we hear is BELIEVE IN YOURSELF, But do you know what it takes to believe in yourself by surrounded a bunch of competitors when is certainly have a blank mind in not knowing what to do with your life and if at all I provide a descriptive answer on how to believe in yourself? The next that pop's up in yourself is why you were born, or know the purpose of your life.

Negativity is what draws you to thinking differently, and absorbing negativity is what transforms you into positive.

Let's say

To Think Differently? It all involves thinking about fresh concepts or simpler answers, correct?

What is the first thing we should do to come up with fresh ideas or to improve things in our country?

It is nothing more than concentrating on unresolved issues. Problems might arise organically or as a result of an existing idea, but the solution needs our intelligence right?

You must draw flaws or bad energy, then use your knowledge to turn it around so that it is on the good side. This calls for you to be an authority on the issue at hand and ongoing brainstorming to deal with potential solutions.

ϷϷϷ

The World Is Not Filled With Selfishness And Cruelties But It Is Just Filled With The Way You Think.

There aren't a lot of cruelties and selfishness in the world. The way you think is all around you in the world.

Your world is shaped by your beliefs since you are a part of it.

Your world is what you think about, not what you see.

What you think influences, what you see.

The world is not a result of the way you think; rather, the world is a result of the way you think.

It is much easier to believe in something real than something fictitious.

The effect of our beliefs has a clear relation to our perception of the world. What we see is the result of what we have. If we believe that the world is horrible, that is exactly what we will have. Every time, we shall witness the worse. If we believe that the world is caring and supportive, then that is exactly what we will experience.

ϷϷϷ

Quote

"*The world is not a result* of the way you think;

rather,

The world is a result of the way you think."

- HARISH REDDY S

TWO
RE-THINK

HARD WORK

What it sounds like in your mind when you hear a word called **"Hard Work"**?

Probably it sounds like a man who is working on his muscles and also least view of working towards accomplishing our goals.

Aren't you spreading negativity by saying HARD WORK?

HARD - It is not as hard as you think it is to achieve your goals.

WORK - It is not the work that you work for it, but it's a habit that you work on it.

Remember it's not a work that you're being hard towards your goal, but it's a habit that is required to achieve your goal, and your habits are infused and biased by your patience and consistency.

And now what does it sound to you when hearing a word called **"Smart Work"**?

Probably now you don't think of a person who is going to Gym, but rather you think about a book, a person with a book, or finding easy and shortcut ways to make your preparation easy.

Practically these above feelings are temporarily Forcing you a step ahead towards the goals you wanted to achieve.

So according to the illusions of the author what do you get to know about this?

Both feelings are temporary unheld commands which cannot be carried for a long stipulated period of time. and this engraved me to polish my thoughts a little bit more to make my readers understand and conclude themselves upon reading.

These feelings are fake and enter and exit like having a cup of coffee.

Is it like forcing you?

Nah, say NO to that.

Seriously motivation is a drug, that gonna spoil you in the end if you haven't created a plan towards your goal

Either hard work or smart work cannot promise to place you on the stage of success.

Do you think so?, Not at all.

You don't require motivation very often but you just need a skill that is patience and consistency to acquire a share in the success stage.

There is a quote saying by Arsene Wenger which says

> *"When You Look At People Who Are Successful,*
> *You Will Find That They Aren't The People Who Are*
> *Motivated*
> *But Have Consistency In There Motivation."*

The motivation comes within you, when you love the work you're doing and the change you're transforming, & this gets you to love the person you're becoming.

You no need to work hard or work smart towards the goals that you want to claim.

You must be natural or develop a personality that fits your goals
Your personality, your perspectives, your vision, your mission, your thoughts everything should be a definition of your goals.

It's not hard work or smart work, it's just you with an empty personality that has to be filled and shaped by your thoughts to drive toward the goals you wanted to pursue.

It is just loving the work, not the hard work or smart work.

ppp

MASCULINITY & FEMININITY

In what perspective our society is male-dominated?

In this modern world, Men's and women's positions in our society are almost equal I believe.

but still, there are some misconceptions about men that, men are dominating feminity.

Of course centuries back Men are often viewed as breadwinners and leaders, while women are frequently limited to domestic tasks. This can give the impression that women are not as respected as males and that our society is ruled by men.

The lives of men and women are unequal treatment is evident in many aspects of life. Women, for example, are frequently paid less than men for doing the same job. Women are also more likely to stay at home with their children, whilst fathers are more likely to work. This can give women the impression that they are not as valued in our culture as males.

We can all agree that male domination existed in the past. but do you still think that male dominance running in this 21st century?

Not exactly but still we can see these centuries-back effects are still awakening the old-fashioned attitude is still very much alive and well in the minds of men and women in places of remote areas

Everyone subscribes to the illusion of male dominance even at present, Like I'm asking, are you really asking me to say the male dominance in this present society or world?

Even with recent developments, it is a well-known reality that women are better cared for by the public than males. Despite men and women being given equal opportunity in today's contemporary society.

With these statistics, it is quite clear who has the dominant voice and who has overwhelming control. Why, then, do we continue to perpetuate the myth that men are dominant?

Consider things from a different perspective.

Women make up the majority of the population, the majority of the workforce, the majority of those with advanced degrees, the majority of those pursuing advanced degrees, and the majority of people earning a livable salary in our country. If, as the old saying goes, "behind every brilliant man there is a woman," then why are men still so vocal about how dominant a part of society they are when it is evident that women are the dominant force?

Most of us have been raised to believe that being a "manly man" means being rough, tough, and dominant. In actuality, men who act in this manner demonstrate weakness and insecurity rather than strength or dominance.

In this world

Most people who are imprisoned are men, most people on the streets are men, most people who commit suicides are men, most people who die in the wars are men, Most people who did crimes are men, and most people who are grading fewer marks are men, most people who have been disrespected are men. is like where is the dominance here?

It is true that men are overrepresented in many aspects of life.

This does not necessarily imply that men are in charge, though in this modern society as well. It is critical to remember that power dynamics in society are complex and cannot be reduced to a single number. In some situations, men may have an advantage, whereas women may be more powerful or influential in others. Social roles between genders are not necessarily fixed, as many of the problems that disproportionately affect men are the result of long-standing structural imbalances.

ᗡᗡᗡ

CASTE

Every system has the same sound, but it is not spoken as such. This is anti-national sentiment. The nation refers to a single nation. The country refers to a single country. The castes refer to the caste that is of one. Although the saying is one, but our lives are not.

As our country says there should be no caste discrimination in our country while also producing caste certificates, differentiating the scholarships for each student, while also reserving some quotas for specific casts even then by all means we are all one. The saying of the sound is one but our lives are not.

These are simply words. These are only policies. However, if you examine society and the people around you, you will notice that discrimination is alive and well. There is no denying that caste discrimination still exists in India. This culture is promoted by the government, schools and institutions, and even members of society.

The author is not against any caste, but he is simply plotting the actual facts of reality and questioning them in order to find valid answers. Despite the fact that we are all one and hail from the same land, our country has far too many castes and people.

We must approach ourselves as one society and never forget that we are one nation, regardless of caste or religion. We hear this message from politicians, our neighbours, and educational institutions. We do believe it, but is this behaviour consistent with our beliefs?

Non-powerful castes are regarded to be less important in our daily life. Others regard them with disrespect. They do not receive equal treatment. Their abilities, feelings, and emotions are not regarded as being equal. They are not treated with the same dignity and respect as others.

Thus, this must end. If we continue to judge individuals based on their classes and beliefs, we will never become a great nation. Until we stop fighting and start supporting one another, we will never have a great country. The only way to build a nation is to start empathizing with people and encouraging them to speak up.

ϷϷϷ

One Who Is Loving & Honest Is Viewed As A Fool, Whereas One Who Can Cheat Others Is Seen As Intelligent.

This is a sad state of affairs because it means that we often distrust the people who are actually the most trustworthy. We view them with suspicion, thinking they must be hiding something.

And we give our trust to those who are more likely to cheat us because we think they must be smart enough to get away with it.

It's a never-ending cycle that can only be broken by changing our attitudes. We must begin to value honesty over intelligence and to give honest people. Only then will we be able to build a society that allows everyone to prosper.

People who are sincere and tell the truth are not respected.

Sincerity is regarded as a fault. Sincerity is considered foolish. Being intelligent is not permitted for being sincere. we live in a world like this.

To succeed in this world and establish yourself as a respected individual, one must be cunning and intellectual.

If you are straightforward, honourable, and ethical, you are a fool. You see, the way the world sees you is both inaccurate and pitiful.

Being open and honest is a sign of wisdom and maturity is considered immaturity to this accused world, whereas Lying, scheming, and cheating, on the other hand, are signs of maturity.

ϷϷϷ

Quote

"*Just Because Something Supports Our Stupidity Doesn't Mean It's True.*

Consume What Is Right Even If It Is Alone,

But

Not Everyone Believes Even If It Is Wrong."

\- HARISH REDDY S

THREE
LIMITATION OF KNOWLEDGE

Rather of introducing more and more theory information, focus should be given on practical knowledge.

Theoretical knowledge is important as it is a base for every rise but it encourages and finally ends up in learning which is of no use. So, changing the education system can help in providing a brighter generation and can create a massive impact on developing our nation.

Besides our educational knowledge, we ignore outside knowledge of other domains because it is in no way related to our persuasion. We only pay attention to the knowledge that is inside our domain of interest or the course we are pursuing.

We only pay attention to the knowledge that is relevant to our field of study or the course we are taking. This is because we consider this knowledge to be more valuable than other types of knowledge.

However, we should also pay attention to other areas of knowledge in order to be more well-rounded. We limit ourselves and our ability to progress when we simply pay attention to knowledge inside our domain of interest.

It is human nature to pay attention solely to information that is relevant to our field of study or the course we are taking. We are constantly flooded with information from all sides, and it's impossible to pay attention to everything. As a result, we naturally concentrate on the information that is most relevant to us.

This attitude can cause us to neglect important information that is outside of our field of expertise. We may fail to see the connections between different fields of knowledge or be blind to advances in other areas that could be relevant to our own work.

It is important to be conscious of this tendency and to seek knowledge from a range of sources. Only in this way can we hope to get a really thorough awareness of our surroundings.

ᚦᚦᚦ

Never Seek help, Unless You tried, made mistakes, learned, and failed to accomplish.

There is a lot of truth to the saying that you should never seek help unless you have tried, made mistakes, learned, and failed to accomplish something on your own. This is because seeking help can often be seen as a sign of weakness, and people who are seen as weak are often not given the same respect as those who are seen as strong.

There's an old saying that goes, "If at first, you don't succeed, try, & try again." And while that's certainly good advice, there's also something to be said for knowing when to seek help. After all, there's no shame in admitting that you need a little assistance, and doing so can actually save you a lot of time and frustration.

Of course, that doesn't mean that you should seek help at the first sign of difficulty. After all, part of the learning process is making mistakes and learning from them. But if you find yourself repeatedly struggling with the same task, it may be time to ask for assistance.

This is not to say that you should never seek help, but rather that you should only seek help when you have truly exhausted all other options. If you seek help too early, you may find yourself in a position where you are reliant on others and not able to accomplish things on your own.

However, if you wait until you have tried everything and failed, then seeking help can be seen as a sign of strength because it shows that you are tried your best and are now willing to admit that you need assistance. even after failing, after seeking help from others learn from them how they are able to solve something that you couldn't able to solve. There is no way that some knowledge is not useful,

Once you seek help from someone, make sure you learn something from that someone so that you should not request the same help again.

Implying this statement in you, helps you to become a continuous learner

ᗁᗁᗁ

Don't only read out-of-date knowledge that doesn't address difficulties in the real world; instead, innovate fresh solutions for the world's challenges.

The world is constantly changing and evolving, and the challenges we face are always changing as well. It is important to stay up-to-date on the latest knowledge and information so that we can address the challenges of the world in the most effective way possible.

However, simply reading and memorizing information is not enough. We must also be able to innovate and create new solutions to the challenges we face.

The ability to innovate is what sets us apart from the rest of the world. It is what allows us to create new technologies and find new ways to solve problems. If we want to be able to effectively address the challenges of the world, we must be able to innovate and create new solutions.

We are constantly bombarded with news and information from a variety of sources, and it can be difficult to sift through everything to find what is most relevant and useful.

It is even more difficult to find reliable and up-to-date information that can help us address the challenges we face in the world today.

With so much information available at our fingertips, it is easy to become overwhelmed and to fall into the trap of only reading out-of-date knowledge that doesn't address the difficulties we face in the present world. This is why it is important to be selective about the sources we consult and to always be on the lookout for fresh solutions to the world's challenges.

There are many ways to find reliable and up-to-date information. One way is to consult experts in the field who are likely to be aware of the latest research and developments. Another way is to use online search engines and social media platforms to find the most up-to-date information and even to solve unsolved case studies with proper research with research tools

It is more necessary than ever in today's world to be innovative and discover new answers to the problems we encounter. We can make a difference in the world and help create a better future for all by being selective about the sources of information we consult and by continually being on the lookout for new ideas.

ܡܡܡ

Quench your need for knowledge beyond your domain and aspirations, and try anything beyond your bounds - you only have one life.

There are many ways to achieve goals in life; it all depends on how badly you want them.
Everyone's route to success will be unique. It's important to realize that you only have one chance to make your life what you want it to be.
Some people spend their entire life searching to decide what they want to do in there lives and others can jump right in without hesitation or guidance.

In any case, it's important to do what you enjoy, take risks, and try new things. We can't all succeed unless we try.

The fear of reaching for something beyond of their line of vision is the only thing stopping us from surrendering to the pleasures of their imaginations.

Anyone wanting more from life should push themselves beyond their comfort zones, as each new experience brings them closer to discovering their true personalities.

"Knowledge is power, and the more one knows, the more influence one has over one's own destiny.

ppp

There is no one right answer to a question, and just because you have one life doesn't mean you have to live with one identity.

The standards that society has for you shouldn't limit you. This may be applied to your values as well as your job objectives.

For example, if you are an artist, there is nothing stopping you from pursuing a career in science.

Similarly, if you have a passion for fixing cars but you don't have the funds to go to college to learn how to become a mechanic, you can still fulfill your passion by taking online courses.

Only you have the authority to choose what is best for you and what will enable you to reach your greatest potential.

ppp

Quote

"Knowledge is power, and the more one knows, the more influence one has over one's own destiny."

- HARISH REDDY S

CHANGE THE WAY YOU ACT!

FOUR

STOP WATERING DEAD PLANTS

You know how many dead plants (people) you have been watering (time, love, and care) throughout your life. We are surrounded by individuals who are selfish, who hate us, and who do not appreciate the relationships we have with them.

Life Isn't that unfair? Why are we all so different? Why are certain people so uncomfortable to be around?

- We all had conversations with people we don't truly like.
- We've had relationships with people that ended in hatred.
- We've worked with people that made us feel uncomfortable, and
- We've had friends who were more of a burden than a blessing. If you're anything like me, you've spent a great deal of time attempting to reach out to these people.
- But why are we making it so difficult?
- Why do we waste time attempting to make someone understand us when they simply don't care?
- Why should we waste our time, feelings, and energy on those who do not deserve us?
- Why are we so forgiving?

You may have heard the old phrase called, **"Pity is for the people who don't deserve it,"**

Which I think is quite true.

It's like water flowing from a mountain peak. & Here the mountain peak indicates those who need our affection and care. And the water, which represents our love and care is flowing downside is wasted on those who are unworthy of it. People who are not worthy of our love and attention are the people who don't love or appreciate you. It's like those who don't even know you exist.

I can say that being able to be yourself without caring about what other people think is the most lovely thing in the world. You are the only one who has power over your own happiness, so don't allow anybody else. You are the only one who can save yourself, indeed be bold and powerful. You are sufficient in your own right, and you do not require anybody else to complete you.

Even i have been through in filtering the relationships in right weight and light weights in my life.

- I've had friends, but I've never had a good time.
- I've tried and failed several times to make friendships.
- I've tried to love, but I've always been disappointed
- I've tried and failed to find happiness and friendship.
- I've tried to live and convince myself to go with the flow of society's beliefs and standards, but I couldn't and I never made it." to live as one of many.
- In my life, I've had some amazing experiences. I've done a lot of things that I'm proud of, as well as a lot of things that I would alter.
- I've made a lot of mistakes and learnt a lot.
- I've had a wonderful time and an even more wonderful heartbreak.
- I've been profoundly loved as well as absolutely heartbroken by someone close to me.
- I've had great moments and bad times.

People don't change unless they want to change.

If a person does not respect you, listen to you, or care for you, he or she will not suddenly start doing these things if you continue to give them a reason to consider you as equal or to count you in their life. *Having feelings for someone who doesn't give you the same vibes back will only make you unclear about your self worth and heartache.*

Never allow someone else take up your thoughts unless you want to invest in them and they deserve it.

If someone decides to leave you, let them go. If the person you're in a relationship with doesn't want to be with you, don't fight for them. If they don't want you, find a better way to love yourself. If they do, they will come back to you. Turn off your caregiver instinct and let them go if they don't appreciate you. Don't let people drain your emotions. If you're in a relationship, learn to love yourself better, it will make you a whole lot happier. You don't need someone to complete you, you are whole on your own. You don't need someone to make you happy, you are happy by yourself. You don't need someone to make you complete, you are already complete.

The next time when you meet someone and their conversation made you to think they are worth of your time, Now don't concentrate on their problems; instead, look for their strengths. Don't try to change someone. Instead, find the good in them and love who they are and don't try to change them into who you want them to be.

Almost everyone understands the importance of their relationships with the people in their lives; you are not a child who does not understand who is right and who is wrong in your life; you are simply afraid of what people will think if you suddenly disconnect from the people who are not good for your mental health.

If you want to find some true and trust worthy, don't spend time with people that are not worthy of your time and energy. Most people do the exact opposite.

- They communicate regularly with those who don't deserve it.

- They spend time with people who are not interested in the same things as them.
- They spend time with people who are not on the same page.
- They waste their time, feelings, and energy on people they don't even like or even hate.
- They don't even mention them in any context.

Follow the quote said by Blaise Pascal - *"If we don't like a person, it is a good reason not to like something he says."* If you meet a person you don't like, it's important to try and find out why you don't like them. Then you will have to decide if they're worth your time. If not, then it's time to move on.

LIFE IS NOT FAIR

- **You Are Right**

When you stated that no one cared about you. That has been revealed to you by life. You have been hurt. You were left just like when you needed someone the most.

- **You Are Right**

Life has taught you not to ask people for help.

- **You Are Right**

When you said that people left you behind You have been abandoned and now you have the feeling that you are not good for anybody.

- **You Are Right**

About being left behind. Life has taught you that and it is ok.
In the journey of my life the only thing I realized is Not to trust anyone. It is true that you have to be careful while trusting anyone,

but you shouldn't be too fearful about it.

Yes, there will be people who will take advantage of your trust, *but there are also people who are worthy of your trust.* No matter how many of the latter category of people you come across, you shouldn't lose hope. **some people are trustworthy, some aren't, and yet some may surprise you.**

ᚦᚦᚦ

The world doesn't owe you anything. The truth is, in this life, you get out what you put in. Nothing more, nothing less.

Anyone who has made a reputation for himself has had to go through it alone, believing that no one is responsible for his accomplishment. Successful people look at their problems as opportunities to better themselves. They never just give up. They keep pushing until they reach their goal. The answer is to be grateful for what you have, and FORCE yourself to be happy with that. You'll be a lot better off if you do.

There is no doubt that everything one does is for one's own good. This could be perceived as a rude statement, yet it is the truth. Expecting a favour from someone who has no personal stake in us is dumb. The best approach is to understand that the person is where he is now it is because of his primary goal is to make himself happy. Making oneself happy may not be the most desirable attribute, but it is necessary to achieve the peak of success and happiness.

I can't tell you how many times I've observed someone break up with friends who were hurting them, only to replace them with people who hurt them just as much. The reason for this is that when we think we have found something unique, we value it very much.

We have a tendency to "water" it until it is well established. Then, when something or someone threatens to take it away from us, we put all of our efforts into saving it. This is a mistake. We need to understand that not all relationships are meant to be in your life just because once you cared.

Watering a dead plant will not bring it back to life, it will only cause it to put more stress on the plant that is still alive. Realize this, and let go.

ᗘᗘᗘ

You can not expect the opinion of others to be a reflection of your own self-esteem. You need to learn to listen to what you think of yourself because this is the only way to know what you should do in life.

There is a theory called downline-up.

Its meaning is that people with higher self-esteem value their opinions higher, so they listen to their own opinions first. People with lower self-esteem are more willing to listen to the opinions of the people around them.

If you want to maintain high self-esteem, then you need to listen to your own opinions first and then the opinions of others. Because in the end you're not entitled to suffer for someone else opinion or decisions on you.

ᗘᗘᗘ

Stay connected to the people who devote more for you not who desire to crave more from you.

The most essential relationships in our lives involve people who care about us and wants us to succeed. These are the people who will be there for us when we need them, as well as those who will assist us in growing and learning.

On the other side, there are people in our lives who are simply interested in taking from us. They could be in friends, family, or even strangers, but all they care about is what they can extract from us. They may take our money, our time, or our energy, but they will never give us anything in return.

It is essential to keep contact with those who care about us while letting go of those who merely want to take from us. Positive relationships will help us grow and prosper, whilst negative interactions will drain us.

The most important people in your life are often those who spend more time and energy to you rather than those who expect more from you. Even if they don't always demand your attention, it's important to maintain communication with those who make you feel loved and supported. People that expect more from you frequently drain your energy and leave you feeling drained. It's critical to establish limits with these people and make sure you're getting what you need from your interactions.

There is a still time before the scribe sits down. I'm still wandering why should we care one's doesn't even think about us . When people left us in pieces all we need to do is the just stop worrying about the situations and the things which doesn't even matter for us . The most beautiful thing in the world is vibing alone and being as you.

You are the hurdle
You are the answer
You are the light
You are the path
Your love will heal you
Your courage will save you
You are enough as you are.

ᗡᗡᗡ

Quote

"People are just people,

not better, not worse, just like you and me.

The whole trust factor is very simple, it just comes down to,

who has your back when you need them!"

\- HARISH REDDY S

FIVE

THE DOER

There have been many successful failures in the world, and I'm not sure if it's due to a lack of confidence, a lack of support, or a fear of others' confidence.

Thinking is not enough, You Must Be A Doer.

Thinking?

Everyone Has An Idea, But Doesn't Have A Constructive Plan?

Most people have a notion of what they want to do with their lives. They may have a general idea of what they want to accomplish, but they rarely have a clear plan for how to get there. This might be annoying because it can feel like you're spinning your wheels and making no progress.

If you find yourself in this scenario, keep in mind that everyone has to start somewhere. It's okay if you don't have all the answers yet. The main thing is to start moving in the right direction. Begin by conducting research and brainstorming to obtain a clearer idea of what you want to do. You may start putting together a plan of action after you have a better understanding.

It may take some time and work to get things started, but pursuing your ambitions is rewarding. Don't be disheartened if you don't have everything figured out yet. Take things one step at a time, and you'll achieve your goal eventually.

ଚ୍ଚଚ

Everyone Thinking about living Big, But Don't Know How?

There are many people who aspire to live a huge, lavish lifestyle. They watch the beautiful lifestyles of the rich and famous and believe that it is something they would never be able to achieve for themselves. They don't realize, however, that it is possible to enjoy a big life without being wealthy. There are several ways to accomplish this.

Traveling is one way to live large. You can travel the world and have experiences you would not have had if you stayed in one place. You can also enjoy all of the advantages that various places have to offer. A great home is another way to live big. You don't have to live in a mansion to have a comfortable, beautiful home that makes you happy.

You can also live the good life by doing things that bring you joy. This could be engaging in hobbies, spending time with family and friends, or caring for yourself. Make a point of doing whatever makes you happy. Finally, you can live lavishly by giving back. This could involve volunteering your time or donating money to causes you care about.

So, if you're thinking about living big, don't let your lack of wealth hold you back. There are plenty of ways to make it happen.

ϷϷϷ

Everyone Thinking About Changing Their Lives, But Don't Know How?

I'm sure we've all had those thinking about ourselves, "I really need to improve my life." But then we talk ourselves out of it just as fast. We convince ourselves that it's too difficult, that we don't know where to begin, or that we're not really ready.

But what if we could learn how to change our lives for the better? What if we could find the courage and the strength to finally make those changes we so desperately want to make?

It's possible. And it all starts with that first, fearful step. It all starts with deciding to change things no matter what.

So if you're thinking about changing your life, but don't know how, take heart. It is possible. And it all starts with you.

ϷϷϷ

Everyone Thinking About Their Future, But Don't Know How?

Many people consider their future but have no idea on how to get there. They may have a rough concept of what they want to do, but they are unsure about how to proceed.

There are a few things you can do to start planning for your future. First, think about what you want to achieve. What are your long-term goals? Once you have a general idea, you can start breaking down the steps you need to take to get there. This can help you feel more focused and motivated.

It is also important to have in mind that your future is not fixed. If something isn't working out, you can always alter your plans. Be adaptable and open to new possibilities. Trust your gut and don't be afraid to try new things. You can do everything you set your mind to with a little planning and work ethic.

ϷϷϷ

Everyone Thinking About Things That They Want To Change In The Society, But Don't Know How?

There's a lot of talk about attempting to improve society these days. But what exactly does that mean? And how can we bring about those changes?

Some people think that change means making things better for everyone. They aspire to see a more just, equal, and fair society. They want to see an end to discrimination and violence, as well as equal opportunity for success for all.

Others may wish to make more specific changes to society. They may wish to increase public education or make it easier for individuals to start their own businesses. They may wish to improve the environment or ensure that everyone has access to healthcare. It is just like as author everyone in this world has some thought of rough idea about changing something on our living.

Whatever your vision for change is, it's important to remember that real, lasting change doesn't happen overnight. It takes time, effort, and dedication to make a difference. However, if we all work together, we can make the world a better place for all.

ᓄᓄᓄ

Everyone Thinking About The Things They Want To Do, But Don't Know How?

There are lots of resources available to assist you in determining how to make your ideas a reality. All it takes is some research and some manual effort. The rest will fall into place once you know how to get started.

I myself strongly believe in us we are more capable and innovative people than the present innovators who are ruling the world now. What's the difference between you and the top most successful entities in the world?

The question is

Are you a capable and creative person? Or is that just your viewpoint? I don't know who you are, but I'm thinking you're a regular person. Because all of us think that we are exceptionally good at what we do.

And these are the reasons why we fail:

1. We have unrealistic expectations of ourselves and others. We have unrealistic expectations of the people we work with. We have unrealistic expectations of our clients and ourselves.

2. We are incapable of dealing with failures and setbacks. We simply give up when things don't go our way. 3. We fail to take the necessary steps. We are continually waiting for the right moment or circumstance.

Whenever you feel overwhelmed or intimidated by someone or something, ask yourself these 3 questions: 1. What am I expecting from myself or others?

2. Am I able to deal with setbacks?

3. Am I taking the necessary actions? If the answers are "no" again and again, you are the limiting factor. Think about it.

The difference is that you're just a thinker if you don't take action upon your thoughts and the Doer is someone who is able to think and take action, but not just limiting the thinking to continous thinking.

How to become a Doer

Are you one of those people who has a million ideas but has no idea on how to put them into action?

If this is the case, you are not alone. Many people never achieve their goals because they lack the confidence to take the initial step. The best part is that it is not as difficult as you may fear.

Here are a few tips to get you started:

1. **Write down your ideas:**

This will assist you in collecting your thoughts and determining what has to be done.

2. **Research your ideas:**

Once you've developed a plan, it's time to begin learning more about your subject. This will allow you to fine-tune your plans and determine what is achievable.

3. **Find a mentor:**

Nothing compares to learning from someone who has previously achieved success. Find someone who can assist you in achieving your goals, or become your own self-idol.

4. **Take action:**

The most important phase is to take action. Don't let your thoughts sit in your head; make them a realistic!

❧❧❧

Quote

"You just limit the thinking to think to feel the pleasure about the someone you want to become

or

something you want to build, or something you want to prove."

\- HARISH REDDY S

CHANGE THE WAY YOU LIVE!

SIX

DON'T SETTLE FOR OKAY LIFE

Is it OKAY to live a life, which is in no way related to you?

Is it OKAY to settle for less, when you're worth more?

Is it OKAY to do a job, which craves no interest in you?

To Be Honest,

Our thoughts are so beautiful about our future life, But making less or zero effort towards the life we want, we just caged ourselves in present with no mission but just blank vision.

All our life, had been hearing these:

- I could not achieve,
- Things I could not have and things I could not do.

I heard these so many times then,

My point is, 'Don't settle for okay life, live your life to achieve everything. Don't let anyone stop you from doing something. Work with dedication and passion and be determined to achieve your dreams.

Nothing in the world can take the place of persistence.

- **Talent will not;** nothing is more common than unsuccessful people with talent.

- **Genius will not;** unrewarded genius is almost a proverb.
- **Education will not;** There are many educated failures in the world. Persistence and determination are all-powerful. The motto "Press On" has solved and will continue to solve the world's issues.

You'll never know if you can do something until you try it. The most important thing you can do is to believe in yourself and believe that you can really do whatever it is your dream is.

If you believe in anything less or settle for less, then you'll never be able to achieve your dream. **Believe it, and the universe will eventually deliver that to you.**

It is not possible to buy success, but if you have the passion to succeed, and never give up, then you will never live your life as a failure. You will achieve everything you desire and be a happy person.

Don't settle for okay life. it doesn't exist. You're born to get succeed, you're capable of everything, don't give up, have passion, and believe in yourself.

ﭖﭖﭖ

You're probably born to be the best at something, so why don't you just do it?

There are countless reasons why people fail to fulfil their life goals, but all of them are fictional; they are only excuses. If you want to be successful, you must overcome your fear and do something you have never done before.

ﭖﭖﭖ

Why would you want to fit in when you were born to stand out?

If you're living a life that is not related to your field of interest, it doesn't mean there is something wrong with you. ***It's just a phase***, which you need to pass through in order to reach your goal. You need to experience various fields before you can decide what really suits you. **Don't be hard on yourself.**

It is never okay to live a life that does not excite you. If you don't find interest in your job, then it is never worth it. If you're settling for less, when you're worth for more, then it is never okay.

But, there is one condition to it: you should not run away from your responsibilities. Just because you're bored with your job, doesn't mean you can neglect your family.

If you don't find your job fulfilling, then give it a thought. Is there a way that you can make it more interesting? If not, then you should consider changing it.

The wise suggestion that I can give you is:

The greatest thing to get valued by the people with whom you're surrounded is by inspiring them.

- Let your discipline build consistency in others!
- Let your progress motivate others!
- Let your success inspire others!
- Let your life should impact others!

If you want to be a role model for others, it is important to be consistent in your own life. This means setting a good example in terms of your behavior and choices. It also means being disciplined in your own life so that you can be a positive influence on others.

Your progress in life can also motivate others to do better. When people see you succeeding, it can inspire them to set their own goals and work towards achieving them. Seeing someone else achieve their goals can be the motivation that others need to get started on their own journey.

Finally, your success can also impact others in a positive way. When people see that you have been able to achieve your dreams, it can give them hope that they can do the same. Your success story can be an inspiration for others to pursue their own dreams.

An inspiring quote from the **late Kobe Bryant** goes like this:

""Resting at the end, not in the middle""

It tells us to work all of the time, not just when we want to. It is about setting high expectations and then trying to reach and sustain them. Every day, we must be content & consistent to show up and put in the effort.

All you've been dreaming or hoping for is at the finish line, don't quit in the middle and feel sad for not getting by what you expected to get in the end!

ᐅᐅᐅ

Don't Live In A Life Sentence Who Wrote By Someone Else For You.

"Life is what happens to you while you're busy making other plans" – John Lennon.

Life is not a movie that someone else has directed for you. You may rewrite the script if you want to live a life that you appreciate.

When you start your journey of getting rich quickly, wealth is at its peak. That's the time when you need to work on yourself. Decide what kind of life you want to live. Write down your goals, determination, and also strategies. You need to be willing to follow the plan.

The most important thing in life is to live it on your own terms, not someone else's. Too often, we allow others to dictate how we live our lives, and as a result, we end up living a life that isn't truly our own. We end up living a life that someone else wrote for us, and it's not a life that we're truly happy with.

ᐅᐅᐅ

Quote

"Inspire people surrounded by you by featuring what you're capable of"

\- HARISH REDDY S

SEVEN

THE CHOICE IS YOURS

Do you feel stuck in your present life?

Perhaps you feel like the choices you made in the past are holding you back?

On the other hand, do you feel like you will accomplish everything you want in the future if you just put in the effort?

Both of these above ideas are true. **Your present life is primarily defined by the choices you made in the past and your future is solely dependent on the choice you make in the present.**

And the quality of your life is defined by the wise choices you made

There are so many opportunities for you to try, so many chances to succeed, and so many doors that can open for you

but the choice is up to you! You need to ask yourself what you want.

Do you want to get good at dancing?

Do you want to be able to play the guitar flawlessly?

Do you want to be a famous writer?

You need to ask yourself these relative questions and then do what it takes to achieve them.

It won't be easy because there's always someone who wants the same thing you do, but as long as you put in the work and never give up on any of your goals, you'll succeed in the end.

We all have a lot to learn from the past. It is the key to our present and future.

- **We can learn from the past**

The past is what has shaped us into who we are today.

- **We can learn from the present**

The present is what we are creating right now.

- **We can learn from the future**

The future is what we hope to create through our actions, in the present.

ᐅᐅᐅ

The choice is yours, not just success but everything that defines the quality of your life.

- **THE CHOICE IS YOURS**

You can choose to be happy or you can choose to be unhappy.

- **THE CHOICE IS YOURS**

You can choose to live in the past or you can choose to live in the present.

- **THE CHOICE IS YOURS**

You can choose to let things bother you or you can choose to let them go.

- **THE CHOICE IS YOURS**

You can choose to be positive or you can choose to be negative.

- **THE CHOICE IS YOURS**

You can choose to be a victim or you can choose to be a survivor.

- **THE CHOICE IS YOURS**

You can choose to be successful or you can choose to be unsuccessful.

- **THE CHOICE IS YOURS**

You can choose to be kind or you can choose to be unkind.

- **THE CHOICE IS YOURS**

You can choose to make the **world a better place**or you can choose to make the **world a worse place.**
THE CHOICE IS YOURS:
You have the power to choose your own destiny. The power to choose is a great gift. It is up to you to decide how you will use that power. Choose wisely. Life is full of choices and it's up to you to make the right ones.
Think about how much time you've spent doing something that you're not passionate about.
Couldn't you have spent that time working on something you really want to do? You have the choice to go after what you really

want or keep doing something that is unsatisfying.

Don't blame others for the things that have gone wrong in your life, It's gone wrong because it was your choices and decisions that drew this bad or negative conclusion.

There is absolutely no individual in this life who is responsible for what's happening in your life, It's Just YOU.

- **You're Your own burden**

You are the only person who can take away your sorrow. You are the only person who can change your life. If you choose to be sad, you have nobody to blame but yourself. If you choose to be happy, you have no one to thank but yourself. The choice is entirely yours.

- **You're your own weakness**

If you're your own weakness, then you have to make a choice.

What choice is that? You must choose to eliminate or reduce the weakness.

For example, if you're a perfectionist and you're your own weakness, you must choose to quit being a perfectionist or, at the very least, try to be less of a perfectionist. Another option if you are your own weakness is to learn more about your weaknesses and attempt to correct them. For example, if you are highly trusting, you can begin to learn how to trust less.

- **You're your own strength**

You always have the option to choose. Do something if you believe in it. If you want to do anything, make it happen. If you want to be successful, you must train tirelessly. To achieve your goal, you must exert effort and work. Nothing will be given to you on a silver platter. Success is not a divine gift.

- **You're your own fate**

It's true. When you realize that everything that has happened to you in life has been a choice you made, you will be more responsible for your actions and will understand that your fate is in your hands.

· **You're your own self**

When you are your own self, you are being the best version of yourself, growing the way you want to grow, helping those you want to help, chasing the ambitions you want to pursue, and making decisions the way you want to make. That is precisely what you desire. You don't want to be like others, and you don't want to be led by others. You want to be yourself while also being happy. That is why you must.

One day you will wake up and realize that there's no more time to do that one thing you always wanted to do. So do it now - Paul Coehlo

As the quote goes you have one life, make the most of it. There are many things you want to do and probably will not get the time to do it. So you have to start now.

You'll wake up one day and realize there's no more time to do that one thing you've always wanted to do. So do it now, while you still have the opportunity. Don't put it off till tomorrow, next week, or next month. Take the first step right now.

Time is a valuable asset that we constantly take for granted. We believe we have all the time in the world to accomplish our goals, yet truly effective runs out. So, while you still have the opportunity, do the things you want to do. and you'll be happy you did.

Don't put off fulfilling your dreams. One day you'll wake up and discover you're getting older and have less time to do the things you've always wanted to do. Do them right away. Make sure your dreams become reality.

ϼϼϼ

Quote

"The past is to learn from, & the future is to build on."

- HARISH REDDY S

EIGHT

RAT RACE

"I would say that success is clearly a state of mind – when you achieve the ability to be content with what you get, then you can be rich, successful and happy in all walks of life."

If you don't create your own life, someone else will hire you for theirs.

When you are living your life for someone else, you are not really living, you are just surviving! You will get everything you want in life if you do the things you want to do. Life is too short to spend it doing things you don't.

RAT RACE occurs when people are driven to work harder and harder in pursuit of an elusive goal - often leading to unhappiness, work-life imbalance, and stress.

You might not be aware of it, but RAT RACE has been running for thousands of years and most people are stuck on the track, running against the clock and earning their daily bread in the process.

The rat race is the common phrase to refer to day-to-day working life. So, you've been calling it a race right? because you are spending your whole day working. **But consider my words you're not in the race, instead, you are running circles around a wheel, while someone else (boss) is sitting in the driver's seat.** What you have to do is get out of the wheel, out of the race and start living your life.

ᐅᐅᐅ

The key to leading a truly fulfilling life is having a mission and living by that mission, whether it be spiritual or material, this is a must for a truly fulfilled life.

I personally believe that to live a fulfilled life, you must have a mission, I don't mean a daily mission, that's just important, but to have a life mission **so that every day you get up you have a purpose for doing so, and you have something to look forward to and strive for.**

Getting a life is a very important thing. Life is all about pursuing what you want. For that, you need motivation, enthusiasm, and inspiration. This can come from everything around you, so be open to it. Open your eyes, ears, heart, and mind to life, and you will be able to **GROW**.

I always ask myself this question and Yes I do live with one identity. I believe that this is the only identity that I have and I am the dominant character in this identity. Also, I live by the fact that the person who is me today, the person who is writing this answer could have been different if I had lived another life. So I am proud of being ME and I have nothing to hide.

I have nothing to comment on or blame your individual life by saying you're not living your life to the fullest,

But what I mean to convey is that get that life that you always had in your mind, It's okay whatever the output at the end you get it doesn't matter. What if you tried and it's worked out?, Then simply being stubborn and dedicating your entire life to just for one identity?

The greatest Quote I ever read from **Ankur Wariko** is that
We have just one life. Why live with just one identity?

Why can't you be an entrepreneur who also creates content?

Why can't you have a day job and also sell your paintings on Instagram?

Why can't you be a professional sports person along with applying for B-schools?

We crave novelty, yet settle for a one-career life.

We crave novelty, yet choose to define ourselves by just one role, one title, one function, and one designation. We have one life. But we don't need to be just one person

The world is concluding your success and failure for you.

Getting a job after graduation is a success

Getting a job with CTC less than your neighbour's is a failure

The thing is the world is already drawn syndromic conclusions for every outcome of your results.

Now It's Your Time To Rewrite It

Let's Rewrite what is true but not believe the wrong just because everyone believes.

- Let's just call a spade a spade
- Let us tell the world the truth without getting in trouble.
- Let us identify the untruths.
- Let's Stop being the blind follower and start being the leader.
- Let's live our life to the fullest.
- Let's embrace the new breed of leadership
- Let's be ourselves
- Let's make your own rules.
- Let's be a rebel.
- Let's not be the sheep in the herd.
- Let's take charge of our own lives.
- Let's do away with the pain.
- Let's break free from the shackles.
- Let's stop blaming others for our failures.
- Let's be honest.
- Let's hold people accountable for their actions.
- Let's question everything.
- Let's not surrender our rights.
- Let's stop following the crowd.
- Let's have the courage to act.

- Let's stand for what is right.
- Let's make the impossible possible.
- Let's fight for the truth.
- Let's be the change we want to see.
- **LET'S START A REVOLUTION...**

Just remember success is a relationship that you have with your own self.

Getting Out of life doesn't mean you need to quit the life you're in now, But it means giving yourself space to find new opportunities to find something that interests you.

1. Try Something New

You don't have to leave your current situation or job to find something new, but you must be willing to explore and take risks. Sometimes the only way to figure out what you really want is to try something new.

2. Let Go Of The Past

What has happened, There is nothing you can do to change. It's time to let go of any lingering resentment, anger, or sadness. These feelings are preventing you from living your best life.

3. Don't Compare Your persuasion with someone else.

Joy is stolen by comparison. When you compare yourself to others, you only set yourself up for failure. Everyone is on their own path and has their own set of talents and gifts for every individual.

ᚦᚦᚦ

Getting Greater later becomes never, Start Now!

It's true, I believe every single person has the potential to achieve great things, but you must learn how to challenge yourself, and start from somewhere.

You don't have to be a world-class or even local celebrity. If you set yourself a goal and work towards it step by step, there's no reason why you can't achieve it, and there's only one way to make it happen is: starting now!

Time is a gift, not a given. We do not receive a new supply of it every day. We should use it wisely

Time is the most valuable commodity we have. But with so many things going on in our daily lives, we tend not to treat them accordingly.

As Benjamin Franklin said, "Truly great men, are all alike in one thing: they are all unlike in precisely the same way."

Remember, when you look back on your life, you want to know that you never settled, that you never lost the fire in you and that you never let the fear of failure stand in your way.

Even if you don't achieve the full potential that others claim you should have reached, you will be happy with your journey. Now is the time to get started. There is a way to reach your dreams, you just have to believe.

Absolutely! Breaking into the top 1% requires relentless hours of work and skill.

Most of the wealthy people you see today worked their way to the top and had to put in the work. **That's why it's vital to start as young as possible. The earlier you start, the longer your chances of building a fortune with minimal difficulty.** It does not matter where you start from, but it's vital to start. Getting rich is not a matter of luck, but rather, a matter of choice!

All of us have the ability to succeed.

However, most of us choose to fail.

- Successful people are successful because they do what unsuccessful people don't do.
- They sacrifice what others won't sacrifice.
- They work more than others and for longer hours.
- They are willing to fail repeatedly until they succeed.
- They are willing to learn from their mistakes.
- They have a strong desire to succeed.
- They have a strong desire to help others.
- They follow a strong plan, which they keep and follow as they strive to reach their goals.

- They are positive, optimistic, and confident.
- They are tireless and persevere, no matter what obstacles get in their way.
- They are never intimidated by the competition.
- They are never intimidated by the odds.

ᐯᐯᐯ

Quote

"*Get Out Of Life, To Get A Life.*"

- HARISH REDDY S

NINE
RE-LIVE

· **THEFT OF YOUR OWN SELF-RESPECT**

Having a positive attitude toward oneself is what it means to love and respect oneself; this involves embracing and appreciating oneself as well as treating oneself with kindness and concern. Setting boundaries and caring for your physical and emotional needs are equally important right?

But also, You Don't have time For Yourself, But you have for others.

But also, Your plans don't matter to you, but others' plans matter to you.

But also, You Don't have time to be productive But have time to act like you're busy.

But also, It Doesn't Matter the schedules you fixed for yourself but you want to prioritize others first.

You assert that you respect and adore yourself. But, do you really?

Let's say you are a working professional

As a working professional, what's your biggest task in a day?

You might need to arrive at work on time as a working employee, wouldn't you think?

You might need to arrive at work on time as a working employee, wouldn't you think? So, on average, you work 8 to 10 hours per day. If I were to ask you, who set these times for you?, You'll probably respond with the CEO of your company or another executive who is in charge of the entire business. Therefore, you are required to work during the time that has been set aside by someone else, and you have obeyed by working during that time and on the tasks assigned to you. Because of this, you cannot skip this cycle and excuse yourself by saying, "I'll do it tomorrow," or "I don't like the scheduled timings," so you must abide by the rules.

So, when it comes to yourself, is it the same? Have you ever assigned yourself a task to complete? and the majority of us failed to finish the task we set for ourselves.

As students, we adhere to the college schedule on a daily basis, but we fail to maintain the same zeal when preparing a timetable for our exams. it's funny right.

As an individual, we failed to respect the decisions that we made for bettering our today and the brighter future of tomorrow, but we are punishing ourselves to follow the transition plan set down by someone else.

Well, you are not the only one who is this, but most of us take this way and it's not uncommon. I am also with you here. I know myself better, we can improve and decide our own goals and make our own rules. we can fight with my addictions, we can be decent, we can be good, we can be happy. But we don't. The thing is, when it's really hard to do something, we feel like that's all we can do. We are not being ourselves. We are being ruled by other people.

We have the power to command ourselves as we wanted to live and we can follow the rules set by ourselves to live a happy life, but we will not. We always give ourselves over to others to be punished based on authority. We always prefer to be ruled by others rather than having the option to rule and lead our lives.

Why do you treat yourself and your decisions with such disregard and disrespect?

It's okay to work in an organization and abide by the schedules they fixed, but also important when it comes to you the things you assigned for yourself, the promise you made to yourself. Schedule yourself. Self-discipline is key for everything. We are all busy. That is true. Be disciplined in what you do, how you do it, how you live, and how you track the passage of time in your life.

One day you will wake up and realize that there's no more time to do that one thing you always wanted to do. So do it now - Paul Coehlo

As the quote goes you have one life, make the most of it. There are many things you want to do and probably will not get the time to do it. So you have to start now.

You'll wake up one day and realize there's no more time to do that one thing you've always wanted to do. So do it now, while you still have the opportunity. Don't put it off till tomorrow, next week, or next month. Take the first step right now.

Time is a valuable asset that we constantly take for granted. We believe we have all the time in the world to accomplish our goals, yet truly effective runs out. So, while you still have the opportunity, do the things you want to do. and you'll be happy you did.

Don't put off fulfilling your dreams. One day you'll wake up and discover you're getting older and have less time to do the things you've always wanted to do. Do them right away. Make sure your dreams become reality.

· THE SPOTLIGHT SYNDROME

You think you're in the spotlight for everybody's view and guess what no one is thinking about what you're doing.

It's crazy how nobody cares about what you're up to, but that's just the way it is.

Sure, people might be interested in what you're doing right now, but in the overall scheme of things, you're only a little fish in a very large pond.

So keep it from affecting your thinking. Don't worry about what other people think of you; just live your life.

You may believe that you are in the public eye, yet no one is paying attention to what you are doing. Life is what it is called, and it's occasionally not all that interesting.

Don't get me wrong, there are people that care about you, but overall, you're only a little component of a much larger picture

No one will peek in to see how your life is going.

No one will peek in to see how well you're enjoying your life.&

No one will peek in to see how bad you're suffering in your life.

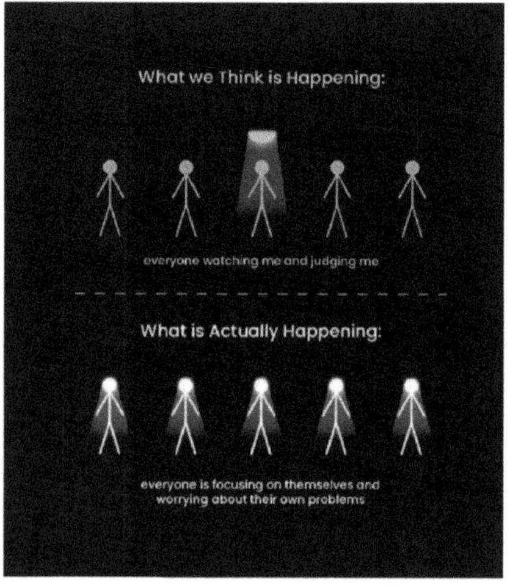

SPOTLIGHT SYNDROME

It's simple to believe that everyone is always observing and evaluating us, but in reality, most people are preoccupied with their own problems to give us much thought.

We often overestimate the importance of our own actions and underestimate the extent to which other people simply don't care. This can lead to feelings of anxiety and insecurity that are out of proportion to reality.

The next time you find yourself worrying needlessly about what other people might be thinking, just keep in mind that they probably aren't even thinking about you.

- Can you imagine how your life would be if you had total faith in your skills and potential?
- Think about how liberated you would feel if you had a high sense of self-worth.
- Can you picture how you would feel if you achieved all of your potential for success?

ᐅᐅᐅ

Quote

"Living all over again is a rebirth of your thoughts and a rebirth of your life."

\- HARISH REDDY S

It's Your Birthday

The world's population is increasing at an alarming rate. It is predicted that the global population would reach 9 billion by 2050. This growth in population has been a significant contributor to the world's hunger and malnutrition problems. Worryingly, the number of starving individuals has climbed to 828 million. It is expected that the number of undernourished people would rise to 1.53 billion by 2050. As of 15th Nov 2022 now we are 8 Billion people around the world, and out of 828 million needy people who are suffering from hunger & undernourishment over every 3 million children who are under the age of 5 are surrendering to death every year.

Wasn't that heartbreaking?

What can we do as individuals to assist lower the number of hungry people in the world, which now stands at 828 million?

So what the author is expressing with the form of the preceding introduction is that you, as an individual, celebrate your birthday every year but also including you 18 million people in this world share your birth date on every single day of the year, Do you believe it soo???

Why can't every one of the 18 million individuals can take the initiative to feed at least 10 to 30 hungry people on your special day?

The 18 million joined project can feed about 540 million needy people on every single day of each individual birthday, and of course, I believe that among those 18 million birthday individuals, there may be those hunger people who maybe a part of that 18 million people's special day.

However, if each person in 18 million accepts responsibility for feeding at least 10 needy people on his or her special day, this equates to feeding more than 540 million needy people every single day, and if this trend continues in the coming years, I believe we will have a hunger-free world very soon.

To feed the poor, we do not need to create a team or form a charity with the exclusive purpose of feeding the needy. Instead, we may dedicate our special day to returning something to the world by being grateful for being born in this world.

Even if we only care for the needy on our special day, our strong commitment and responsibility to having occasional care for the needy are more than enough to save our humanity, that's enough to fill someone's stomach, that's enough to see a starved smile, that's enough to receive blessings from them, that's enough to be grateful for our existence.

Let's prove ourselves to ourselves that we are humans with humanity.

Let's care of others on our special day.

This a tiny idea from an author that still believes if you're kind enough, even if you're poor, go and feed at least one person who is hungry, the smile and blessings of that person will make you understand the importance of your existence.

❧❧❧

Conclusion

The moment you decide that you desire more for yourself, the entire universe begins to change in your Favour. Your proclamation, command, intentions, visions, and prayers start the process of creating the new reality. All you have to do is make a decision and never look back.

This gift of life was bestowed onto all of us. We were all born with unique skills and abilities. However, the majority of us do not use them. We settle for what we know and are afraid to dream of anything different. We dream yet most of us are terrified of change.

We dream yet are terrified of change; we dare to imagine of changing the world but afraid of society. You understand what is right for you, what may be right for society or the world, and what changes are required to recreate our civilization.

It is you that initiates a new beginning!

For the rest of our being let us Re-Make & Re-Live our lives...

▷▷▷